MODERN FUNDAMENTALS 4 FINGERPICKING SCALES

or
How I Learned to Ignore Dogma
& Embrace the Free Stroke

by
Brad R. Thomson, M.M.

ISBN 978-0-9892302-0-9

Copyright © 2013 by Brad R. Thomson
All Rights Reserved
No part of this publication may be reproduced, stored in a retrieval system, or transmitted,
in any form or by any means, electronic, mechanical, photocopying, recording, or otherwise,
without prior written permission of the author.

Photography by Joel Marsh
All Rights Reserved

About the Author

Brad R. Thomson is a classically trained jazz guitarist. He has a Bachelor of Music degree from the University of Nebraska at Omaha and a Master of Music degree from the University of Denver's Lamont School of Music. Brad has been playing music professionally in a variety of idioms since he was 15.

As a working Omaha guitarist, Brad performs mostly in clubs, at weddings, and corporate parties. While playing with local jazz legend Luigi Waites' band, some notable performances include: opening for the Dirty Dozen Brass Band at the Omaha Summer Arts Festival, Taste of Omaha, Jazz On The Green, and A&E television's Jackpot Diaries. In 2002 Brad was hired to play with Multi-Grammy award winning, The 5th Dimension, at Omaha's Fourth of July Memorial Park Concert. He was an adjunct professor of guitar at Creighton University before opening a local music store, Garage Guitar. Brad uses the alias Pierre Reinhardt when playing in his gypsy jazz ensemble, Manouche Moustache. Recently, he has begun to sing standards while playing fingerstyle jazz guitar.

Forward

As both a jazz and classical guitarist I have often encountered difficulties bridging the gap between the scalar facility of using a pick versus that of using the fingers. Breaking through the dogma of traditional technique was no easy task. I humbly present a method that has alleviated the dilemma for me.

This is not a book of scales, but rather an approach to the mechanics of the plucking hand in scalar applications.

The 4 in the title of this book is intentional. Just as the human is able to run with the use of both legs, the cheetah is able to run at incredible speeds with the use of four legs. It is this line of thought, in accordance with ergonomics and economics, which has propelled my technique.

The exercises within will initially have no intentional musical context. Each fundamental technique will then be used in a deliberate harmonic application. Upon being indoctrinated, the guitarist will have the basic skill set needed for the implementation of most scale like passages. Enjoy!

Introduction

The musical examples in the book are simultaneously written in both the staff (treble or g clef) and tablature (tab) format. The measure lines are only used to show distinction from one string to the next.

Strict observance of the picking hand nomenclature is the most important aspect of this book.

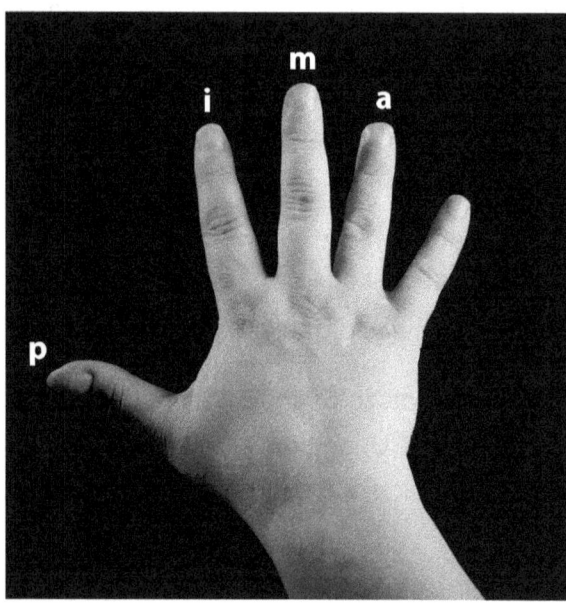

Thumb (pulgar) - p

Index (indice) - i

Middle (medio) - m

Ring (anular) - a

As the alternate title of the book states, this is a modern methodology in utilization of free strokes.

For those guitarists who are not familiar with the term "free" and "rest" stroke:

Rest stroke
When you play the first string, for example, with "i", and follow through the plucking motion and come to rest on the second string.

Free stroke
When you play the first string, again with "i", and the finger leaves the string and immediately contracts into the hand.

The philosophy of playing a scale with free strokes versus rest strokes is a controversial topic. My summation is, whatever technique works best for you is the best for you. This book is a pathway to what works best for me. I have sincere hope that the concepts herein help you. Trying something new can transform or reaffirm your beliefs. Find the positive in everything.

Though it is not within the scope of this particular book, I do utilize the rest stroke in other applications. I have not abandoned it.

Rhythmic Primer

There are many approaches musicians take when practicing with their metronomes. In a nutshell, slow and even leads to fast and even. Guitarists, however, seem to ignore the rhythmic scale, which is playing at different subdivision levels of a beat. It is especially important.

Playing two notes per string makes one want to play two notes per beat. Playing three notes per string makes one want to play three notes per beat. So on and so forth.

Applying the rhythmic scale to each exercise is a method to avoid the sympathetic trap of wanting to play rhythms based on the number of notes per string. As much as I adore polyrhythmic approaches and beat displacement, I am compelled to refrain from opening a larger can of worms.

Rhythmic Scale - moving through subdivisions of a single beat

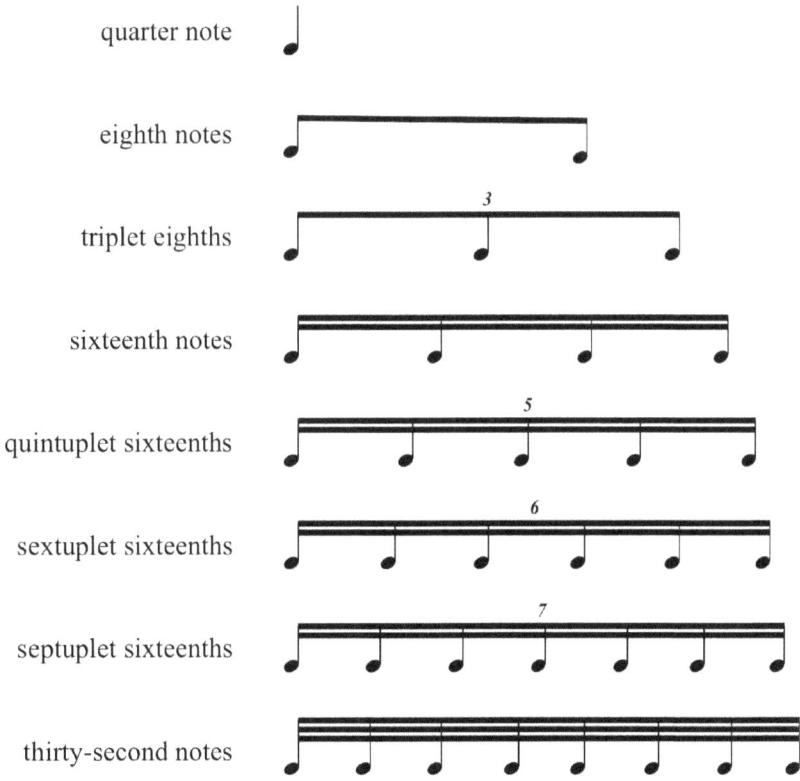

Practice in any way you can think of.
Typically 1,2,3,4,5,6,7,8,7,6,5,4,3,2,1

Picking Hand String Positions

With respect to anatomical alignment, the following picking hand positions are utilized in the linear application of the free stroke:

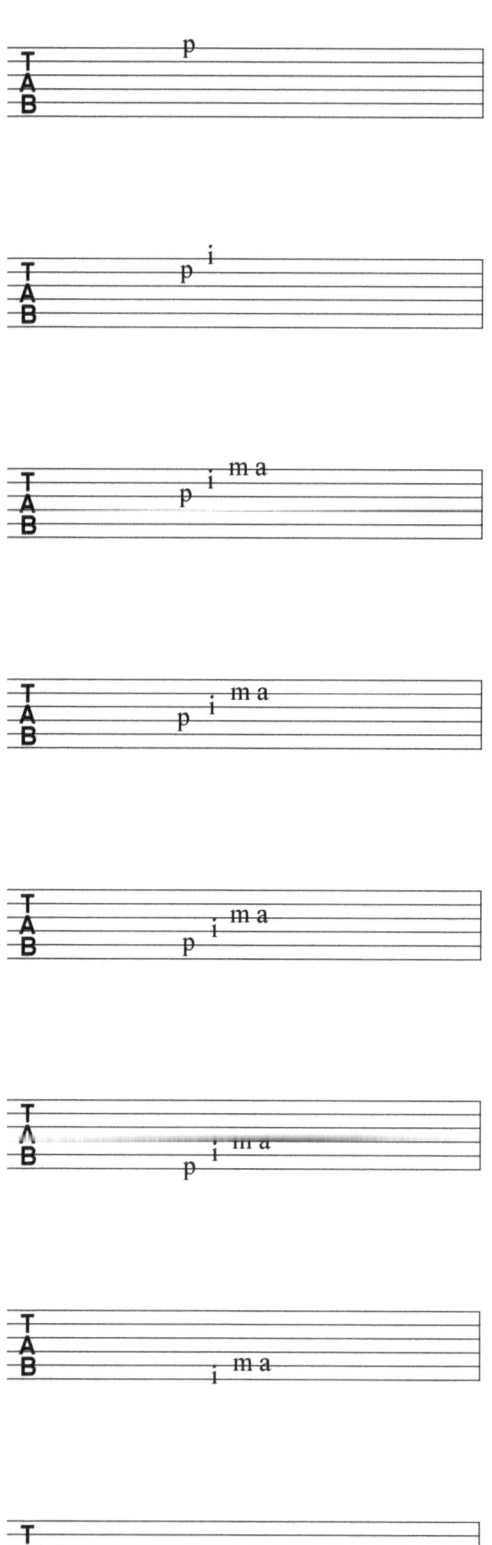

Notes and Tips as You Play Each Exercise

- Observe the double bar and take a breather.

- Building muscle memory takes time and repetitions. Never be in a hurry. Give it time and let it grow.

- I prefer to play in a long sleeve shirt. It is easier to maintain the same form with my fingerpicking arm while shifting through the different picking hand string positions.

- The classical guitarist will have a compelling moment in picking philosophy from the very first example. Hang in there. Try all the exercises. What I thought was initially cumbersome became extremely economical and ergonomic.

- Practice with patience and persistence.

Section 1 Two Notes per String

Exercise 1

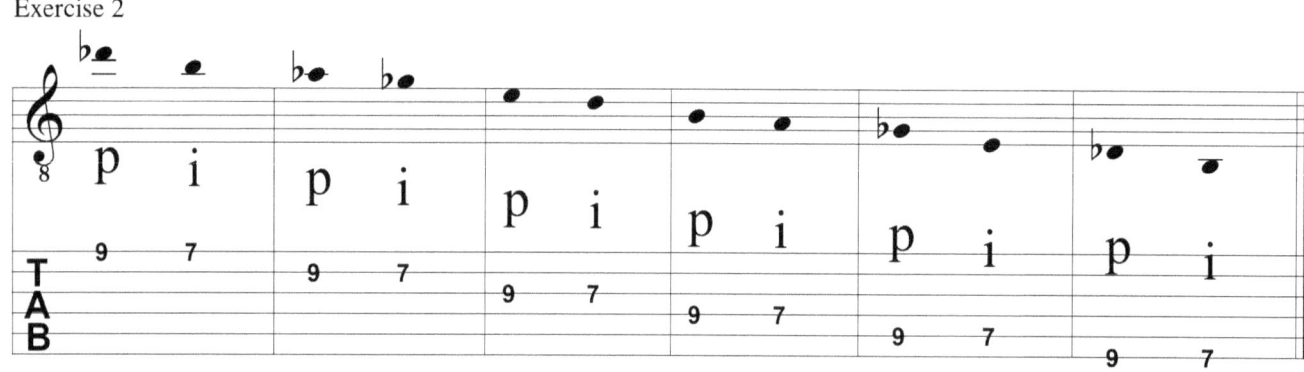

Exercise 2

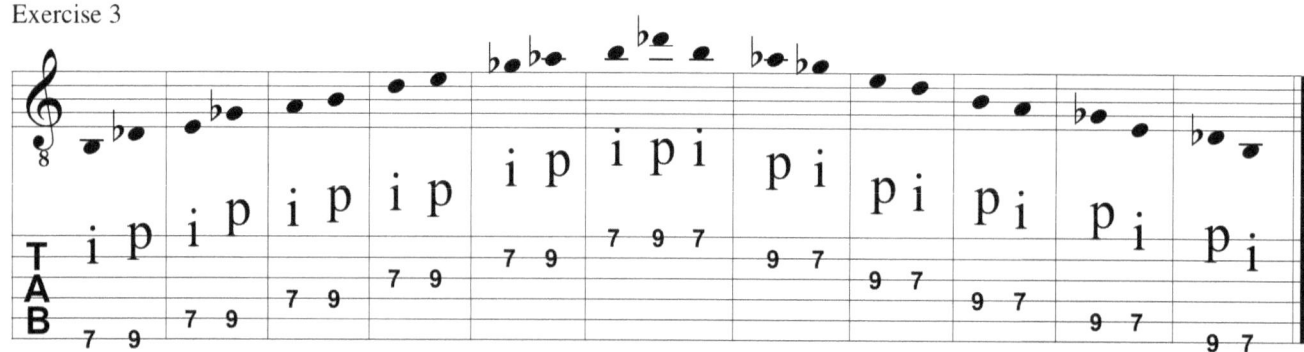

Exercise 3

Exercise 4

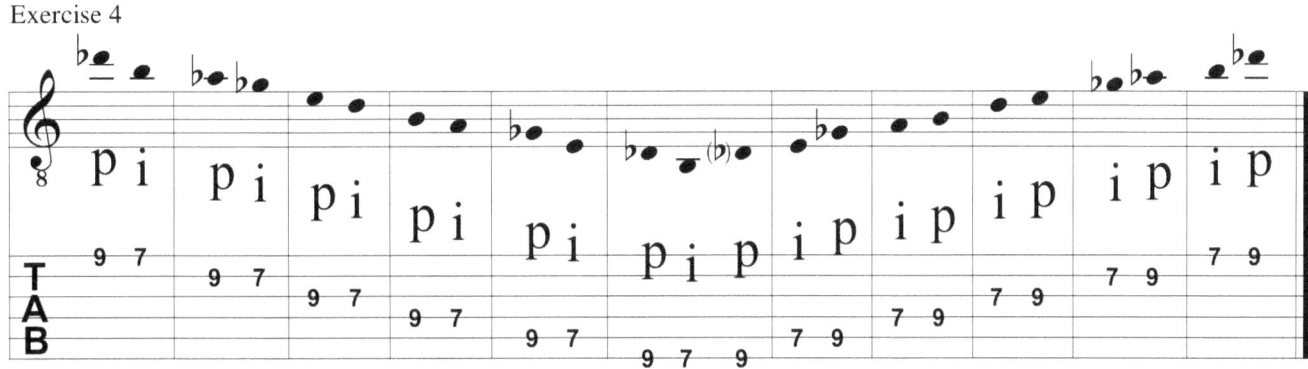

Exercise 5

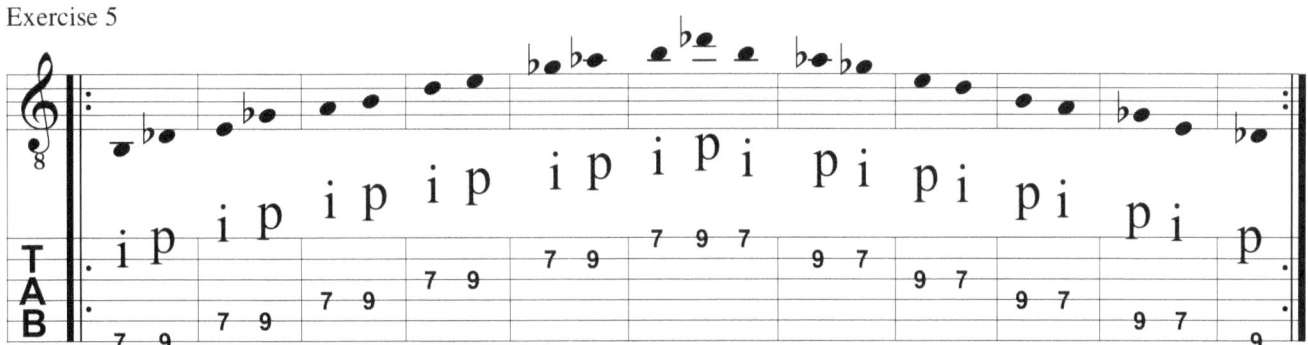

Section 1 *cont.* Harmonic Application of Two Notes per String with the Minor Pentatonic Scale (common form)

Exercise 6

Exercise 7

Exercise 8

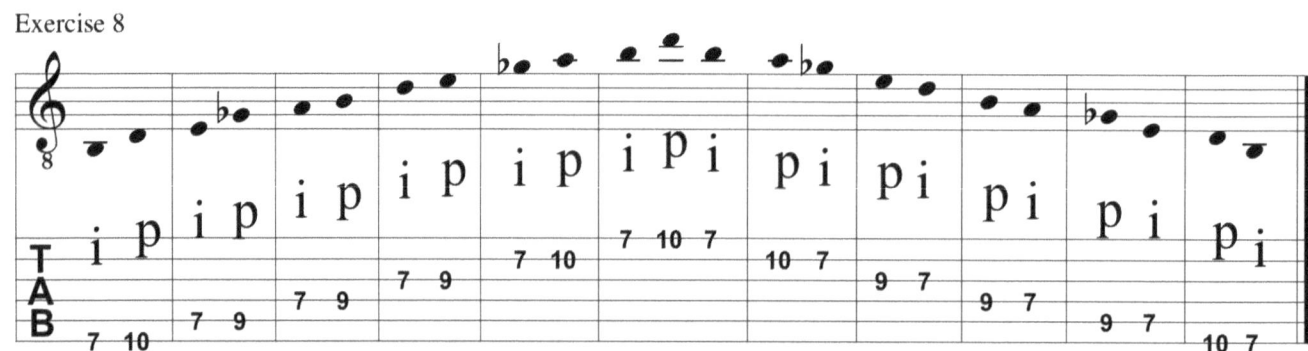

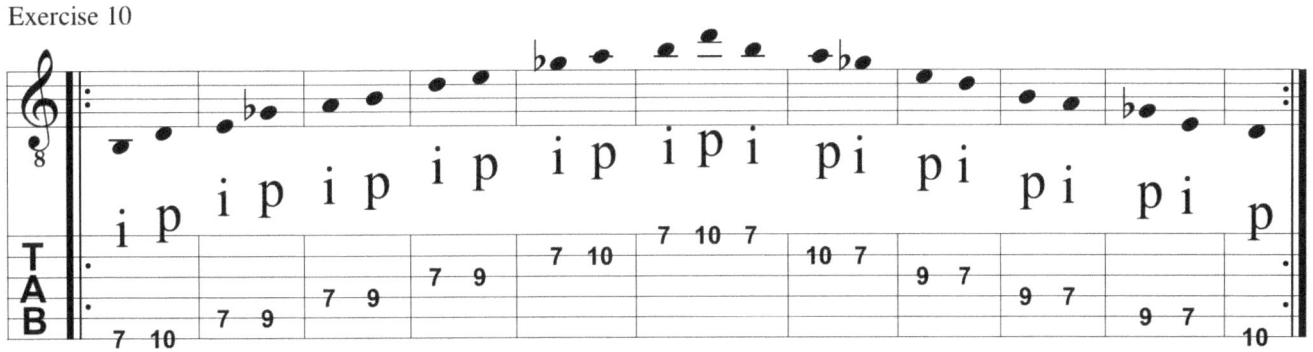

"Apply to any scale form where there are two notes per string (minor pentatonic, major pentatonic, etc.)"

Section 2 — Three Notes per String

Exercise 11

Exercise 12

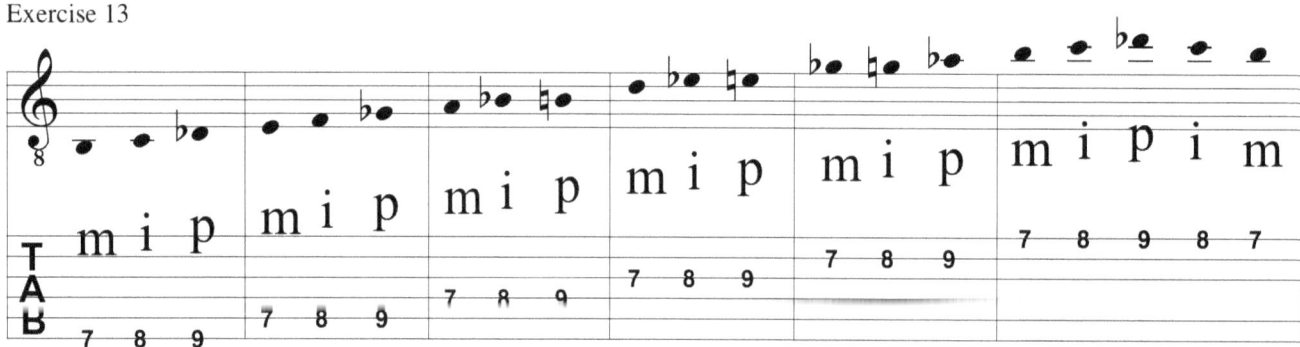

Exercise 13

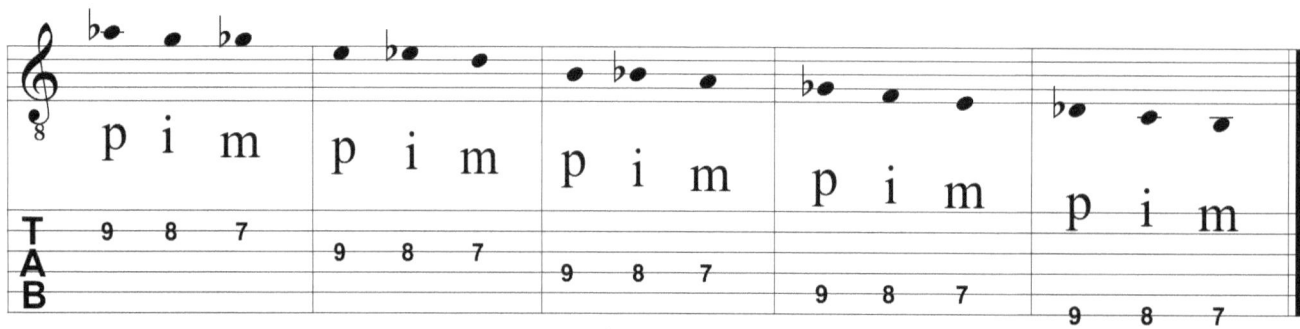

Exercise 14

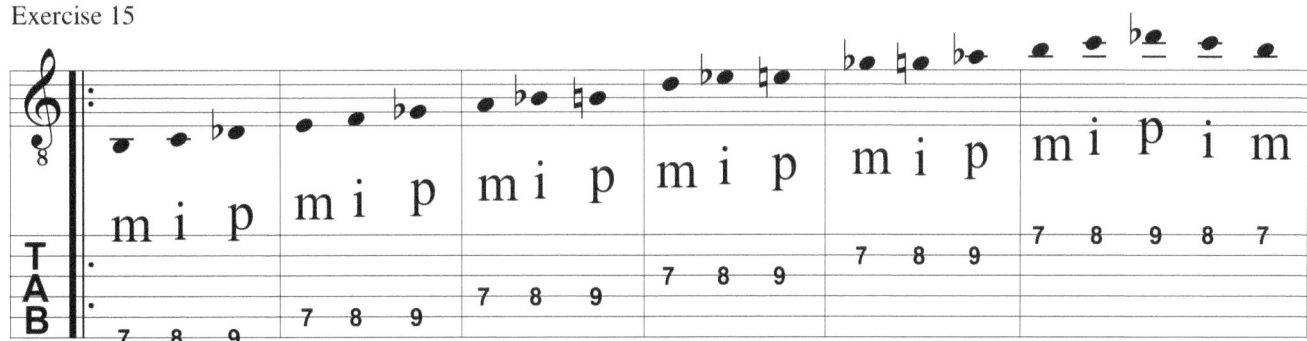

Exercise 15

Section 2 cont. Harmonic Application of Three Notes per String with the Major Scale

Exercise 16

Exercise 17

Exercise 18

Exercise 19

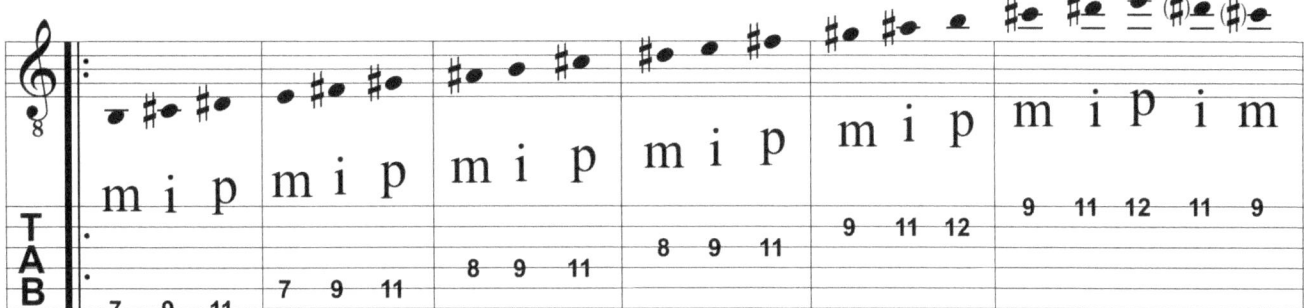

Exercise 20

"Apply to any scale or mode that utilizes three notes per string"

Section **3** Two and Three Notes per String in Alternation
• This is only one of many possibilities. Explore and be creative!

Exercise 21

Exercise 22

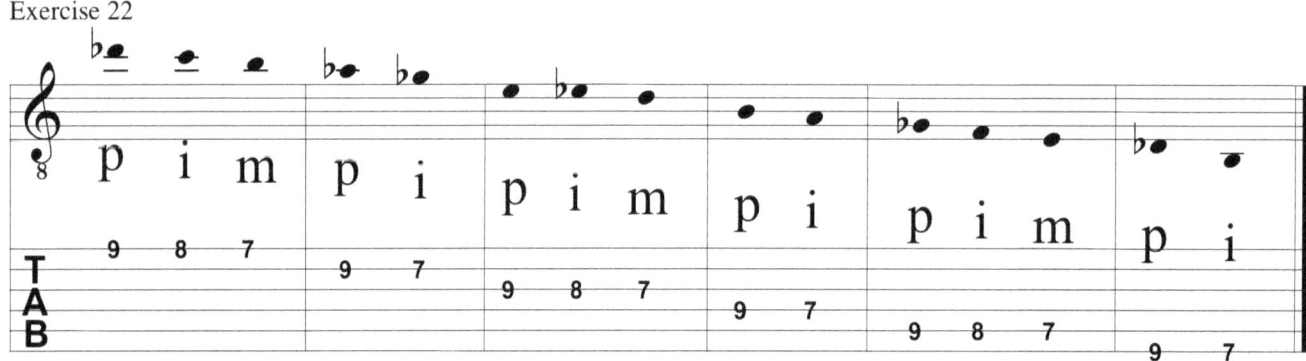

Exercise 23

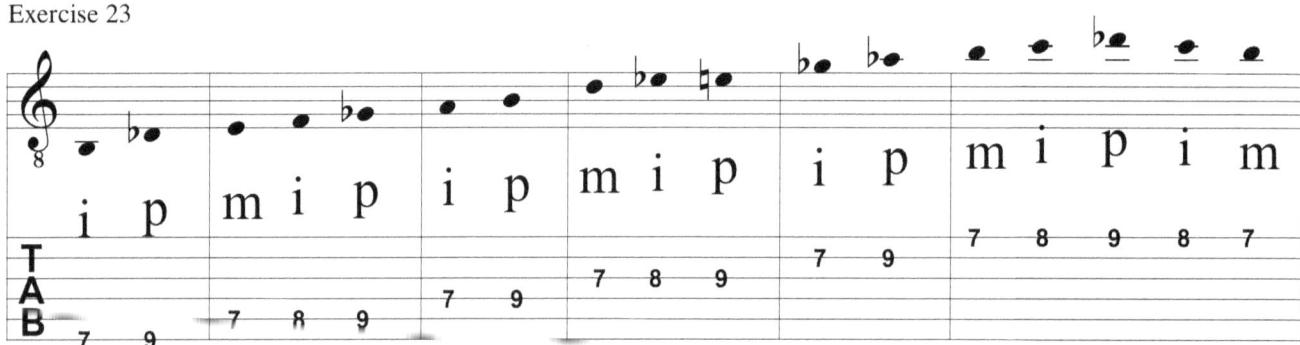

Exercise 24

Exercise 25

Section 3 cont. Harmonic Application of Two and Three Notes per String in Alternation with the Blues Scale (common form)
• This is only one of many possibilities. Explore and be creative!

Exercise 26

Exercise 27

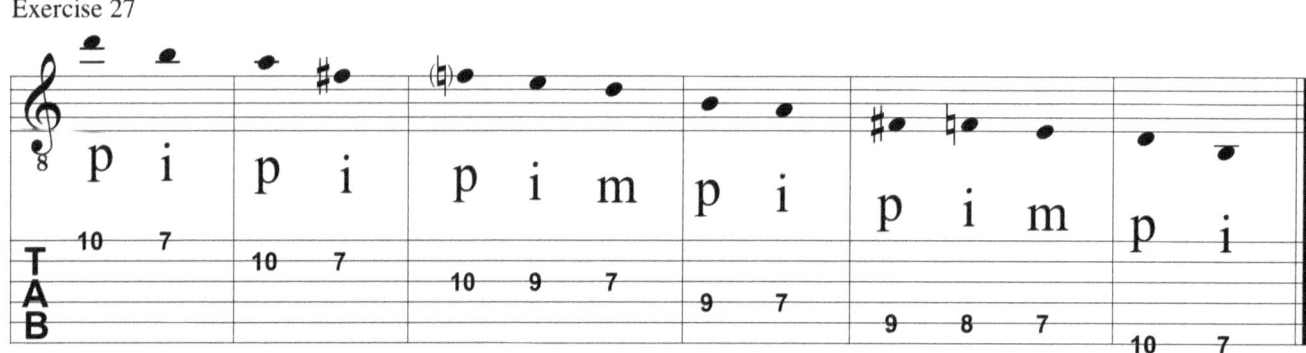

Exercise 28

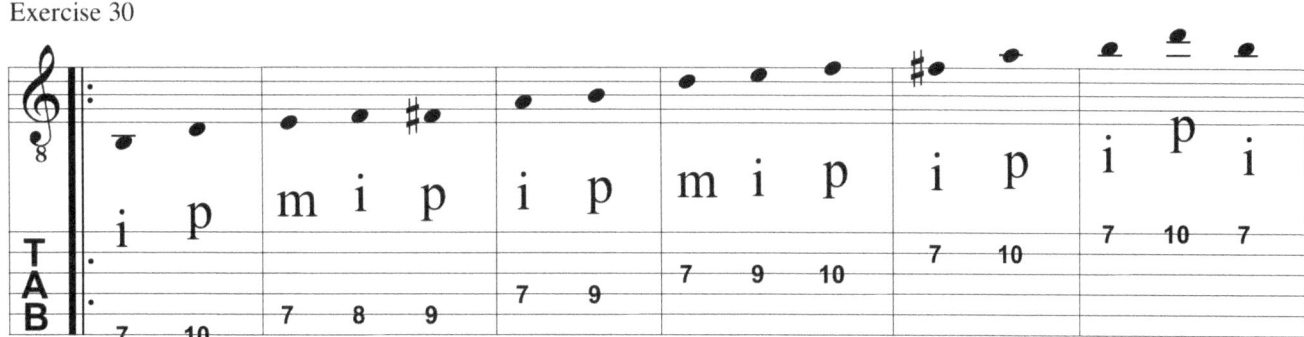

Section 3 *cont.* Harmonic Application of Two and Three Notes per String in Alternation with the Major Scale (common form)
• This is only one of many possibilities. Explore and be creative!

Exercise 31

Exercise 32

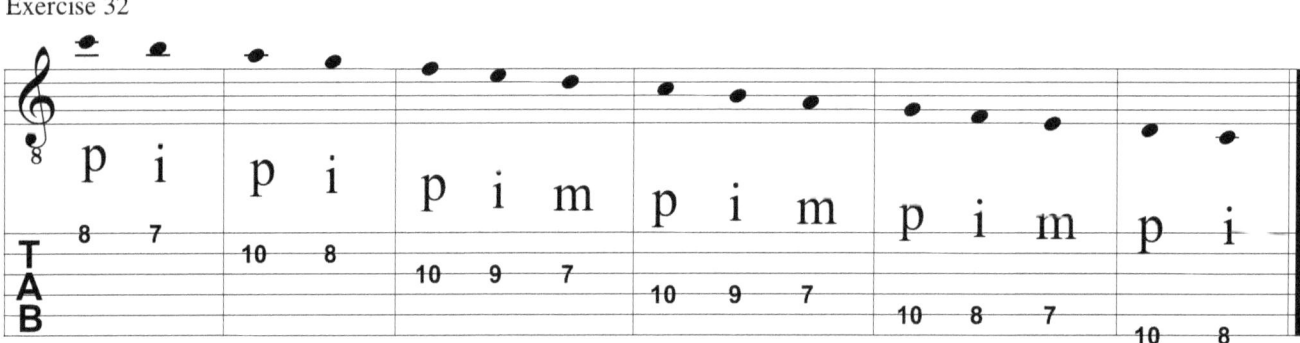

Exercise 33

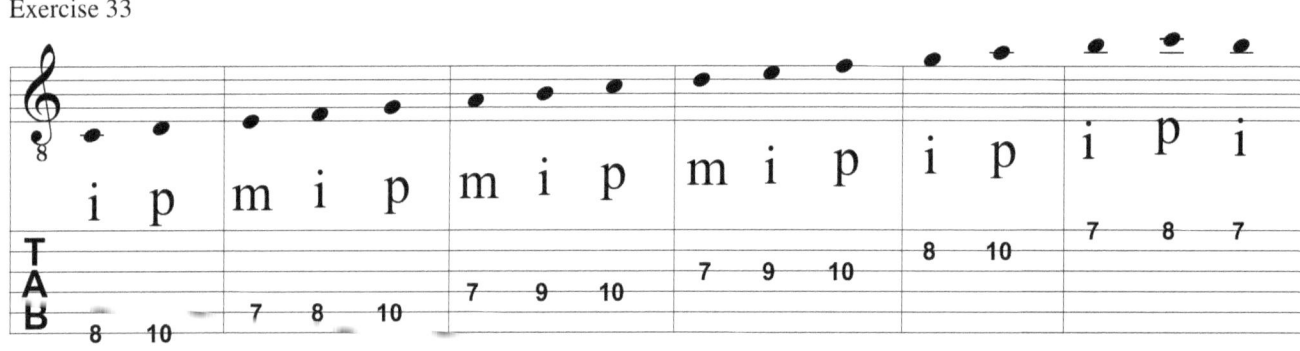

Exercise 34

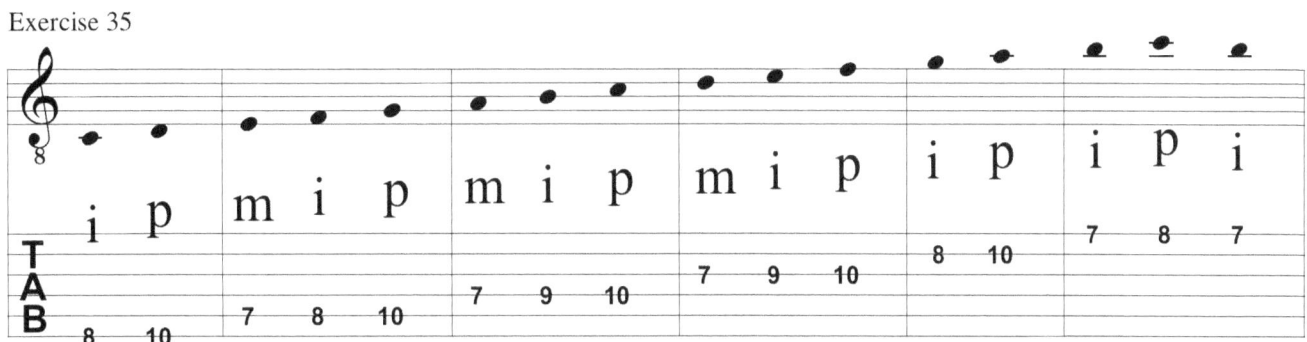

Exercise 35

"Apply to all scale forms that utilize two and three notes per string"

Section 4 — Four Notes per String

Exercise 36

Exercise 37

Exercise 38

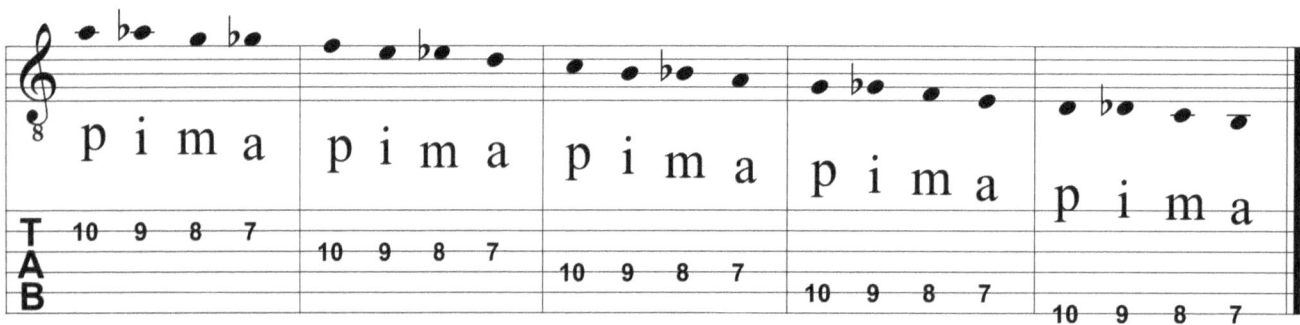

Exercise 39

Exercise 40

Section 4 cont.
Harmonic Application of Four Notes per String with the Chromatic Scale

Exercise 41

Exercise 42

Exercise 43

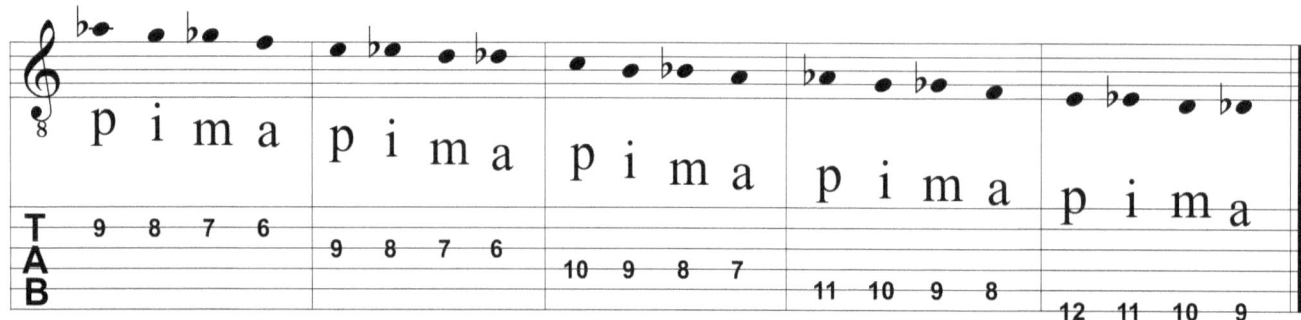

Exercise 44

Section 4 cont. Harmonic Application of Four Notes per String with the Major Scale (not so common)

Exercise 46

Exercise 47

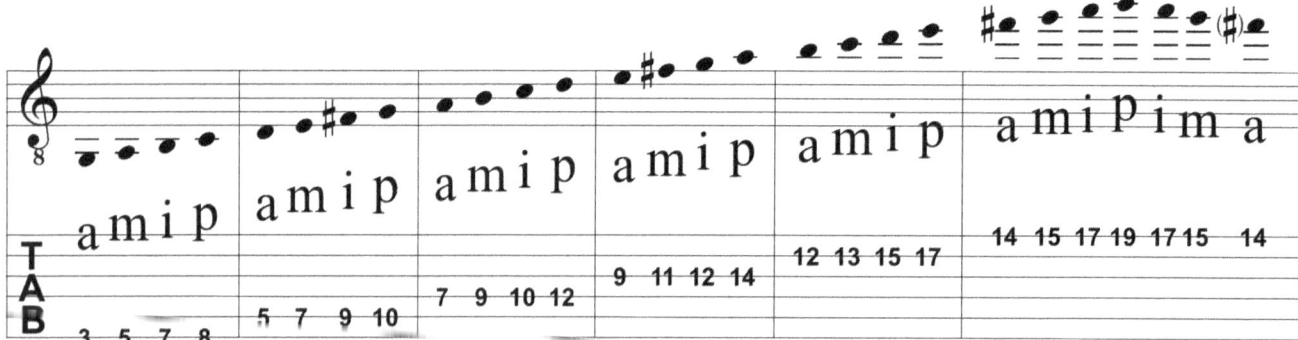

Exercise 48

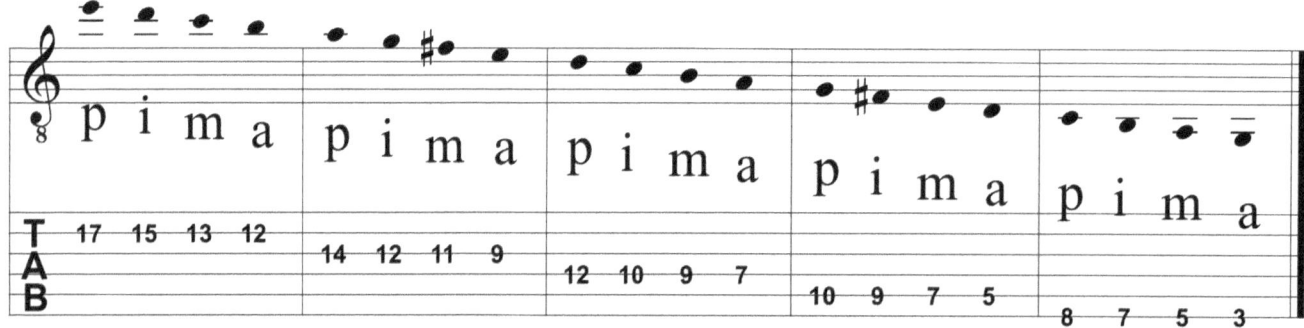

Exercise 49

Section 5 — Alternation of Two, Three, and Four Notes per String
This is only one of many possibilities. Explore and be creative!

Exercise 54

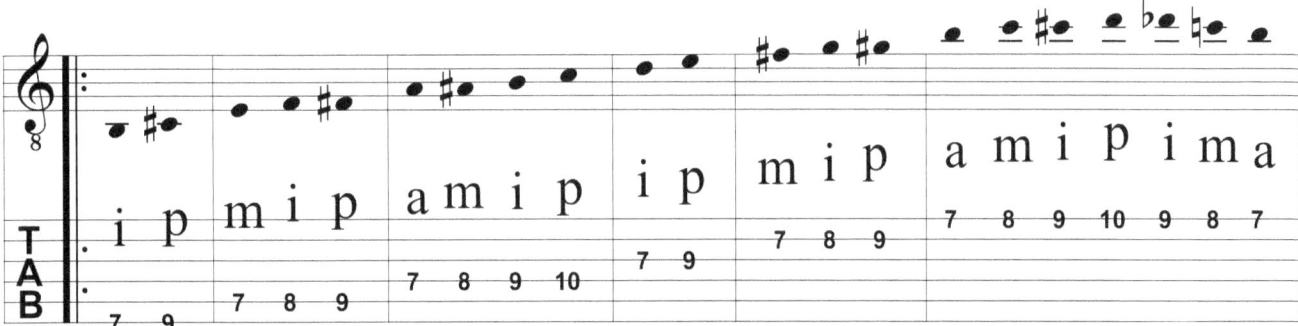

Exercise 55

Section 5 cont.

Harmonic Application of Two, Three, and Four Notes per String in Alternation with the Bebop Major Scale (common form)
• This is only one of many possibilities. Explore and be creative!

Exercise 56

Exercise 57

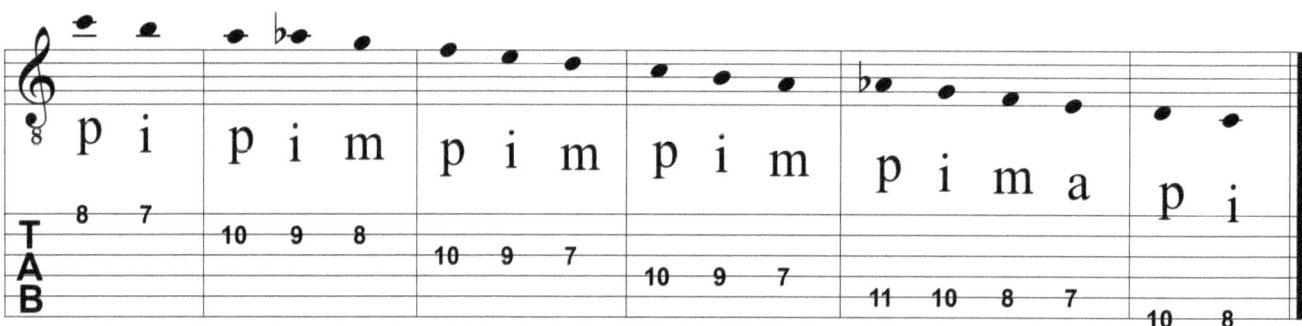

Exercise 58

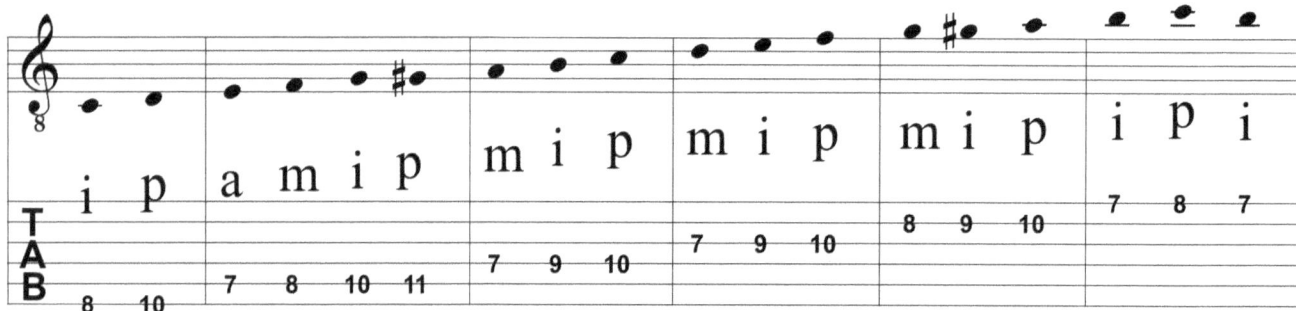

Exercise 59

Exercise 60

"Apply to all scales that involve alternation of
two, three, and four notes per string"

Section 6 Five Notes per String

Exercise 61

Exercise 62

Exercise 63

Section 6 *cont.* Five Notes per String

Exercise 64

Exercise 65

Section 6 cont. Picking Hand Application of Positional Chromatic Scale

Exercise 66

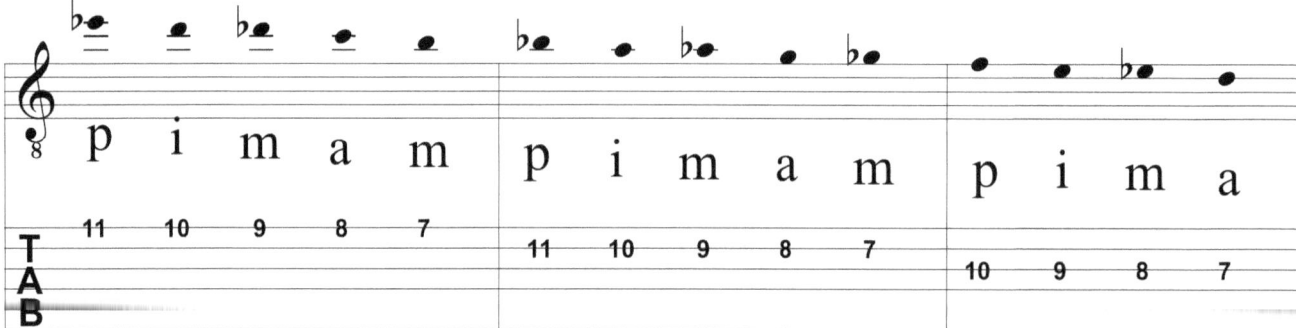

Exercise 67

Exercise 68

Section 6 cont. Picking Hand Application of Positional Chromatic Scale

Exercise 69

Exercise 70

Epilogue

Congratulations! You've made it this far. Your journey, however, has only just begun.

Technique is something that needs to become second nature. Its application must become one without conscious thought. The only physical task when playing is embracing freedom of movement-movement with little to no effort.

Intuition is your greatest ally. After going through the different examples the classical guitarist needn't bother writing in a fingering for a scalar passage. The goal is that the hand will simply produce the desired results. The improvising guitarist will only have to employ legato technique because he/she wants to, not out of necessity.

It is the constant responsibility of an instrumentalist to master various techniques. To transcend beyond their respective instrument and play music is the true goal. May this book be one small aspect that a fingerstyle guitarist absorbs so he or she can enrich the life of the listener.

Acknowledgements

I am ever grateful to all of my teachers, my guitar playing friends and colleagues, my students, everyone I have played music with, and everyone whose music I have enjoyed.

Saxophonist extraordinaire Curt McKean who generously translated my handwritten music notation to a proper format for this book. Long live Luigi Inc!

A special thank you to my family. They are the true litmus test of my music. When they say it is good, I know it needs improvement. When they are enthusiastic and their words struggle to describe emotion, I know I am improving.

My greatest appreciation goes to my wife, Julia. She is the most beautiful counterpoint to everything in my universe. She has taught me the meaning of life...Love.